The Flavours Series

CRANBERRIES

ELAINE ELLIOT

Photography by Julian Beveridge

FORMAC PUBLISHING COMPANY LIMITED
HALIFAX 1999

PHOTO CREDITS:
All photographs by Julian Beveridge except where noted below:
Ocean Spray International Services Inc.: p 5, top & bottom
Chuck Russell, *The Vancouver Sun*: p 4, top

PARTICIPATING ESTABLISHMENTS:
The Actor's Retreat Café, Victoria, PEI
Aux Anciens Canadiens Restaurant, Quebec City, PQ
Blomidon Inn, Wolfville, NS
The Briars Resort, Jackson's Point, ON
Catherine McKinnon's Spot O' Tea Restaurant, Stanley Bridge, PEI
Charlotte Lane Café and Crafts, Shelburne, NS
Cranberry Cove Inn, Louisbourg, NS
Dundee Arms Hotel, Charlottetown, PEI
Halliburton House Inn, Halifax, NS
Inn at Bay Fortune, Bay Fortune, PEI
Inn on the Cove, Saint John, NB
Inn on the Lake, Waverley, NS
The Jubilee Cottage Country Inn, Wallace, NS

Kaulback House Historic Inn, Lunenburg, NS
La Maison Dining Room, Halifax, NS
La Perla Dining Room, Dartmouth, NS
Libertine Café & Kitchen, Halifax, NS
Little Shemoque Country Inn, Port Elgin, NB
Mountain Gap Inn, Smith's Cove, NS
Murray Manor Bed and Breakfast, Yarmouth, NS
The Prince Edward Hotel, Charlottetown, PEI
Seasons in Thyme, Summerside, PEI
Shadow Lawn Inn, Rothesay, NB
Sunshine on Main Cafe and Bistro, Antigonish, NS
Tattingstone Inn, Wolfville, NS
Whitman Inn, Kempt, NS
Wickwire House, Kentville, NS

This book is dedicated to the many chefs and innkeepers who have generously provided recipes and to my patient family.

Copyright © 1999 by Formac Publishing Company Limited

All rights reserved. No part of this book may be reproduced or transmitted in any form or by any means, electronic or mechanical, including photocopying, or by any information storage or retrieval system, without permission in writing from the publisher.

Formac Publishing Company acknowledges the support of the Department of Canadian Heritage and the Nova Scotia Department of Education and Culture in the development of writing and publishing in Canada.

Canadian Cataloguing in Publication Data
Elliot, Elaine, 1939-
      Cranberries
      (The Flavours series)
      Includes index.
      ISBN 0-88780-473-X
1. Cookery (Cranberries).   I. Title.   II. Series.
TX813.C7E44 1999   641.6'476   C99-950063-5

Formac Publishing Company Limited
5502 Atlantic Street
Halifax, N.S.
B3H 1G4

Distribution in the United States:
Seven Hills Book Distributors
1531 Tremont Street
Cincinnati, Ohio 45214

CONTENTS

INTRODUCTION

$\mathcal{F}$or years cranberries were only used for the traditional sauce that accompanies turkey at Thanksgiving and Christmas, just a few weeks after the fresh crop has arrived at the market. This book opens up a new world of gourmet delights. From chutneys to soups, from innovative main dish entrées to delectable desserts, the cranberry has come of age!

In this ninth cookbook in the Flavours series, the chefs of selected inns and restaurants in Eastern Canada share their cranberry recipes. Photographer Julian Beveridge visited many of these establishments to capture the dishes as they are prepared.

HISTORY

Cranberries, sometimes known as bounce-berries or crane berries, are grown on trailing vines in boggy areas of North America. While berries are easily found in the wild, commercial cultivation has now made the cranberry harvest a viable part of the food producing industry.

This small, seed-filled oval berry should be firm to the touch, smooth, and a medium to deep red colour when ready for harvesting. In Europe, the lingonberry, which is also of the *vaccinium* genus, is found growing on shrubs in the cold mountainous regions of Scandinavia and Germany. Gourmets of both continents have traditionally served these tart berries with roast fowl or venison. Today, with greater understanding of the healthy properties of this tiny berry and chefs willing to develop new recipes, cranberries have emerged into the culinary limelight.

Cranberries ripen in late autumn and are generally harvested during September and October.

Store fresh berries in plastic bags in the refrigerator for up to one month. Wash berries carefully before using, being sure to discard the tiny stems and soft or blemished fruit. Cranberries freeze very well and may be stored up to 1 year. Package them, unwashed, in airtight, heavy-weight plastic bags. Frozen cranberries should be rinsed and cleaned, then used without thawing. They are suitable for most recipes calling for fresh berries.

Cranberries contain a large amount of natural pectin, thus making them an ideal ingredient for sauces and chutneys.

Sweetened and sun-dried cranberries, called for in some of these recipes, are available year-round in most supermarkets. They add an interesting dimension to sauces and baked goods or may simply be eaten as a nutritious snack.

A one-cup serving of fresh cranberries contains 47 calories and is an excellent source of Vitamin C. They are very low in calories and sodium and are a source of fibre.

BREAKFAST DISHES

*W*hat better way to start your day than with a tantalizing cranberry treat!

◀ *Flavour-filled Cranberry Orange Muffins in the breakfast room
of Kaulback House Historic Inn, Lunenburg, NS*

CRANBERRY ORANGE MUFFINS

MOUNTAIN GAP INN, SMITHS COVE, NS

This is a delightfully tart muffin. The orange juice concentrate combines well with the cranberries. I suggest you double the recipe because they freeze well.

1 cup cranberries, coarsely chopped

1 egg, beaten

2/3 cup milk

1/3 cup butter, melted

3 tablespoons orange juice concentrate

1/2 teaspoon vanilla

zest of 1 orange

1 3/4 cups flour

2 1/2 teaspoons baking powder

1/3 cup sugar

1 teaspoon salt

Preheat oven to 400°F.

Mix together cranberries, egg, milk, butter, orange juice concentrate, vanilla and zest.

In a separate bowl, sift together flour and baking powder and stir in sugar and salt. Add the milk mixture to the dry ingredients, stirring just enough to blend. Spoon into paper-lined muffin tins and bake until golden, 20–25 minutes.

Yields 12 muffins.

RED RIBBON CRANBERRY COFFEECAKE

CRANBERRY COVE INN, LOUISBOURG, NS

Guests at the Cranberry Cove Inn , which overlooks Louisbourg Harbour, are served this cranberry delight, warm from the oven, the creation of innkeeper Carole Swander.

Topping

1/4 cup flour

2 tablespoons sugar

1 tablespoon butter

Cranberry Sauce

2 cups cranberries

1 cup sugar

1/2 cup water

Batter

2 cups flour

3/4 cup sugar

1 1/2 teaspoons baking powder

1/2 cup butter

1 egg, beaten

1 teaspoon vanilla

3/4 cup milk

2 cups cranberry sauce

Preheat oven to 350°F.

Place topping ingredients in a small bowl and using a pastry blender, combine until ingredients are the size of small peas. Set aside.

To prepare sauce, combine cranberries, sugar and water in a saucepan over medium high heat. Bring to a boil, reduce heat and simmer until berries are cooked and sauce has thickened, approximately 20 minutes. Cool and purée.

For the batter, place flour, sugar and baking powder in a large bowl. Cut in butter with a pastry blender until mixture resembles coarse meal.

In a separate bowl whisk together egg, vanilla and milk. Add to flour mixture, stirring only until batter is moist.

Spread half the batter over the bottom of a greased 9-inch quiche pan.

Place cranberry sauce in a bowl and beat with a fork until smooth. Spread over batter in pan. Top with remaining batter, spreading with a spatula to avoid disturbing the cranberry sauce. Sprinkle with topping and bake 20 minutes or until a toothpick inserted into the centre comes out clean.

Serves 6-8.

CRANBERRY ALMOND PANCAKES

WHITMAN INN, KEMPT, NS

Situated near "nature's treasure"—Kejimkujik National Park—guests at the Whitman Inn are offered substantial breakfasts often featuring local berries and pure maple syrup.

2 cups flour

1 tablespoon baking powder

1/2 teaspoon salt

1/4 cup large flake rolled oats

2 eggs, beaten

1 3/4 cups milk

1 cup fresh or frozen cranberries

1 1/2 cup sugar

1/2 cup slivered almonds

1 teaspoon vanilla

pure maple syrup

In a large mixing bowl combine flour, baking powder, salt and oats. Stir in eggs and milk. In a food processor combine cranberries, sugar, almonds and vanilla, processing until finely chopped. Stir cranberry mixture into pancake batter.

Pour 1/3 cup of batter onto a hot griddle. Cook pancakes until surface bubbles. Flip and cook the other side. Serve warm with butter and pure maple syrup.

Yields 15–20 pancakes.

A hearty breakfast of Cranberry Almond Pancakes as served at Whitman Inn, Kempt, NS ▶

CRANBERRY, ORANGE AND BANANA FRUIT FLIP

THE PRINCE EDWARD HOTEL, CHARLOTTETOWN, PEI

Chef Paul Paboudjian first developed this flip as a refreshing low-fat drink to serve for cocktail parties as an alternative to alcoholic beverages. He notes that it is equally delicious served as a "breakfast on the run."

1/2 cup fresh cranberries

1/2 cup freshly squeezed orange juice

1/2 cup sliced banana

1/2 cup skim or low-fat milk

1/2 cup plain yogurt

1/2 cup low fat vanilla ice cream

sugar, optional

2 orange segments, 6 fresh cranberries and 2 slices banana, as garnish

Incorporate cranberries, juice, sliced banana, milk, yogurt and ice cream in a large blender and process on high until smooth. Add sugar, as desired, and pour into parfait glasses.

Serve garnished with a skewer of orange segment, cranberries and a thick slice of banana.

Yields 2 servings.

PINEAPPLE CRANBERRY BREAD

There are those times when a leisurely breakfast lasts so long it approaches the "brunch" hour. This tea bread is designed for those who like to indulge their sweet tooth while lingering over another cup of coffee.

3/4 cup sugar

3 tablespoons butter

1 egg

2 cups flour

1/2 teaspoon baking soda

1 teaspoon baking powder

1/2 teaspoon salt

3/4 cup undrained crushed pineapple

1 cup cranberries, coarsely chopped

1/2 cup almond slivers

Preheat oven to 350°F.

Using an electric mixer cream together the sugar, butter and egg.

In a separate bowl sift together the flour, baking soda, baking powder and salt. Add to egg mixture alternately with crushed pineapple, beating until combined. Stir in cranberries and almonds. Pour into a well greased 9 x 5-inch loaf pan and bake 60 minutes or until a toothpick inserted in the centre comes out clean. Let stand in pan 10 minutes before turning out on a wire rack. Yields 1 loaf.

CHRISTMAS MORNING CRANBERRY MUFFINS

KAULBACK HOUSE HISTORIC INN, LUNENBURG, NS

The aroma of sugar and spice does make all things nice—especially when Karen Padovani of Kaulbach House Historic Inn pulls these delicious muffins from her oven.

1 cup cranberries

1/4 cup sugar

1 1/2 cups flour

1/4 cup sugar (2nd amount)

2 teaspoons baking powder

3/4 teaspoon salt

1/2 teaspoon cinnamon

1/4 teaspoon ground allspice

1 egg, beaten

1/4 teaspoon grated orange zest

3/4 cup orange juice

1/3 cup butter, melted

1/4 cup walnuts, chopped

Preheat oven to 375°F.

Coarsely chop cranberries, sprinkle with 1/4 cup sugar and set aside.

In a medium-sized bowl stir together the flour, second amount of sugar, baking powder, salt, cinnamon and allspice.

In a separate bowl, combine egg, orange zest, juice and melted butter. Add all at once to flour mixture, stirring to moisten. Fold in prepared cranberries and nuts.

Fill greased muffin cups 3/4 full and bake until golden, approximately 15–20 minutes.

Yields 12 medium muffins.

APPETIZERS, SOUPS AND ACCOMPANIMENTS

*S*ome like their cranberries stewed into a sauce in the traditional manner, and some like them hot! In this section you will find something for every taste.

◄ *Chef Peter Woodworth's Chilled Cranberry and Raspberry Soup served at LiberTine Café and Kitchen, Halifax, NS*

CHILLED CRANBERRY AND RASPBERRY SOUP

LIBERTINE CAFÉ & KITCHEN, HALIFAX, NS

Chef Peter Woodworth marries the flavours of cranberry, raspberry and apple in this tangy chilled soup. Either fresh or frozen berries may be used in this recipe.

2 cups cranberries

2 cups apple juice

1 cup raspberries

1 tablespoon sugar

1 tablespoon lemon juice

1/4 teaspoon cinnamon

plain yoghurt or sour cream as garnish (optional)

Place cranberries, apple juice, raspberries, sugar, lemon juice and cinnamon in a blender and process on high until puréed. Pour into serving bowls and garnish with a dollop of yoghurt or sour cream. Serves 4.

CRANBERRY–ONION RELISH

INN ON THE LAKE, WAVERLEY, NS

This is a simple to prepare relish which can be stored up to one week, covered and refrigerated. It is an excellent accompaniment to roasted chicken or turkey.

1/4 cup onion, chopped

1 small garlic clove, minced

1 cup whole cranberries

3 tablespoons sugar

1 tablespoon water

1 teaspoon cider vinegar

Coat a saucepan with cooking spray and place over medium high heat. Add onion and garlic and sauté until tender. Add cranberries, sugar and water, bring to a boil. Cook 3 to 5 minutes or until mixture has thickened. Remove from heat and stir in vinegar.

Store refrigerated in an air-tight container. Serve at room temperature.

Yields 1 cup relish.

TATTINGSTONE INN'S CRANBERRY CHUTNEY

TATTINGSTONE INN, WOLFVILLE, NS

Innkeeper Betsey Harwood prepares this chutney recipe using many different Annapolis Valley fruits. She says the cranberry rendition offered in this recipe is a wonderful addition to a holiday turkey dinner!

8 cups cranberries

4–5 cloves garlic, minced

1 cup raisins or dried currants

3 cups packed brown sugar

1 1/2 teaspoon ground ginger

1 teaspoon dried mustard

1 1/2 teaspoon cinnamon

1 teaspoon crushed chili peppers

1/3 teaspoon salt

1 cup cider vinegar

Combine all ingredients in a large stainless steel saucepan and bring slowly to a boil. Cook, uncovered and stirring occasionally, reducing heat as chutney begins to thicken, approximately 1/2 hour.

Bottle in sterilized jars for immediate use or process in a water bath for longer storage.

Yields 6 cups.

THE DEFINITIVE CRANBERRY SAUCE

This recipe has stayed with me over the years, although I have no recollection of its source, however, it is the most flavourful of cranberry sauces.

2 cups water

zest of 1 large orange

2 cups sugar

2/3 cups orange juice

1 tablespoon lemon juice

3 cups fresh cranberries

1 tablespoon brandy or orange liqueur

In a small saucepan combine water, sugar and zest. Cover, bring to a boil, then reduce heat and simmer 30 minutes. Drain, reserving zest and 3/4 cups of cooking liquid.

In a large pot stir together the reserved liquid, sugar, orange and lemon juice; bring to a boil stirring often. Add cranberries and zest, boil vigorously, stirring constantly until berries burst, approximately 5 minutes.

Remove from heat and stir in brandy or liqueur.

Yields 3 cups.

COUNTRY PÂTÉ WITH CRANBERRY COMPOTE

BLOMIDON INN, WOLFVILLE, NS

Chef Keith Bond serves this elegant compote over pâté as a quick and easy appetizer.
He also serves it as an accompaniment to roast pork or poultry dishes.

1 cup water

2 cups sugar

2 cups cranberries

2 cups chopped apple

8 ounces pâté

toast points or assorted crackers

In a large saucepan combine water and sugar, stirring to dissolve. Over medium high heat bring to a boil, reduce heat and simmer 5 minutes. Add cranberries and apple and return to a boil. Remove from burner, cool, then refrigerate.

Serve pâté with cranberries and toast points or assorted crackers. Serves 6.

A simple but elegant appetizer Country Pâté with Cranberry Compote from the chef of ▶
Blomidon Inn, Wolfville, NS

BRIE BAKED EN CROUTE WITH CRANBERRY SAUCE

LITTLE SHEMOQUE COUNTRY INN, PORT ELGIN, NB

Innkeeper Petra Sudbrack of Little Shemoque Country Inn provides her puff pastry recipe for this delightful appetizer. The less confident cook could use one half of a package of frozen puff pastry.

2 cups cranberries

1 cup sugar

1/2 cup water

Puff Pastry, recipe follows

1 pound wheel of Brie, chilled

1 egg, whisked together with 1 tablespoon water

In a saucepan over medium high heat combine cranberries, sugar and water. Bring to a boil then reduce heat and simmer until berries are cooked and sauce has thickened, approximately 20 minutes.

On a lightly floured surface roll out pastry dough. Using Brie as a guide, cut a circle approximately 3 inches wider than the cheese. Brush edges with egg wash to ensure seal. Wrap cheese in pastry, pinching edges together to form a collar around the cheese. Pastry scraps may be used to make decorative pastry rounds for the top. Chill Brie uncovered 30 minutes.

Preheat oven to 425°F. Bake Brie on a cookie sheet in the middle of the oven until pastry is puffed and lightly browned and cheese is melted, approximately 20–25 minutes. Remove from oven and let stand on cookie sheet for 20 minutes. Serve with cranberry sauce.

Puff Pastry

1 cup cold butter

1 1/2 cups sifted flour

1/4 teaspoon salt

1/2 cup cold water

Cut butter into 14 cubes and place in freezer for 30 minutes. Place flour and salt into a food processor and pulse to combine. Add the butter and pulse 3 or 4 times, there should still be large lumps of butter. Run the machine for 5 seconds while pouring the water through the feed tube, then stop the machine. Turn the mixture out on to a lightly floured, cool work surface and gather into a ball. Flatten slightly, wrap in plastic wrap and place in freezer to chill for 10 minutes.

Roll out the dough into a rectangle. Fold in thirds, bringing one end down to cover the middle, then fold the other end over it. Repeat, and again chill the dough for 30 minutes. Roll and fold the dough as above, wrap in plastic wrap and chill at least 30 minutes or up to 3 days before using.

A colourful combination Baked Brie en Croute with Cranberry Sauce from ▶ Little Shemoque Country Inn, Port Elgin, NB

CRANBERRY CONSOMMÉ

THE JUBILEE COTTAGE COUNTRY INN, WALLACE, NS

A garnish of whipped cream and dill sprigs crown this ruby-coloured soup which, depending upon the whim of the chef, may be served hot or chilled.

2 cups chicken stock

1 bottle cranberry cocktail, 40-ounce size

2 green onions, sliced

1 orange, cut in thick slices

4 whole cloves

salt and pepper, to taste

1/2 cup heavy cream (35% m.f.), whipped

chopped fresh dill or parsley sprigs

6 cinnamon sticks

1/2 cup fresh cranberries

Combine stock, juice, onions, 2 slices of orange, and cloves in a stock pot and bring to a boil. Immediately reduce heat and simmer for 10 minutes. Strain soup through a fine sieve and serve garnished as desired.

To serve hot: ladle soup into bowls, add a few cranberries, a dollop of whipped cream and a sprinkling of chopped dill or parsley. Stir with a cinnamon stick.

To serve cold: cover soup and refrigerate several hours. Fill pastry bag with whipped cream and pipe rosettes onto a foil-lined baking sheet, freeze. At serving time, top each bowl of soup with a few fresh berries and whipped cream rosettes and sprinkle with dill or parsley sprigs.

Serves 6.

*Served warm or chilled, the addition of cinnamon sticks adds flair to ▶
Cranberry Consommé from Jubilee Cottage Country Inn, Wallace, NS*

SPICY CRANBERRY PEAR CHUTNEY

WICKWIRE HOUSE, KENTVILLE, NS

Innkeeper Darlene Peerless prepares her spicy chutney in the early autumn when local cranberries and pears are in the market.

4 cups fresh cranberries

1 cup seedless golden raisins

1 2/3 cups sugar

1 tablespoon cinnamon

1 1/2 teaspoon ground ginger

1/4 teaspoon ground cloves

1 cup water

1 medium onion, chopped

2 medium pears, peeled and chopped

1/2 cup celery, chopped

1/2 cup slivered almonds, optional

In a large saucepan combine cranberries, raisins, sugar, cinnamon, ginger, cloves and water and bring to a boil. Reduce heat and cook 15 minutes, stirring occasionally. Stir in onion, pears, celery and almonds. Continue to cook an additional 15 minutes or until mixture thickens.

Bottle in sterilized jars and store refrigerated for immediate use, or process with a water bath for extended storage.

Yields 6 cups.

Innkeeper Darlene Peerless of Wickwire House marries the flavours of cranberries and ▶
pears in her Spicy Cranberry Pear Chutney at Wickwire House, Kentville, NS

MAIN DISHES

*I*n this section our chefs have outdone themselves with their originality! Here you will find an array of main course entrées, from seafood and poultry to pork or venison dishes, each enhanced by cranberries.

◄ *Versatile pork tenderloins are stuffed with Red Onion and Cranberry Confit at Sunshine on Main Café and Bistro, Antigonish, NS*

PORK TENDERLOIN STUFFED WITH RED ONION AND CRANBERRY CONFIT

SUNSHINE ON MAIN CAFÉ AND BISTRO, ANTIGONISH, NS

Owner-Chef Mark Gabrieau suggests that the confit in this recipe may also be used to stuff pork chops before grilling or used as a glaze over baked pork chops.

1 cup diced red onion

1 1/2 teaspoon butter

1 tablespoon liquid honey

2 tablespoons red wine vinegar

2 tablespoons red wine

1 tablespoon black pepper corns, ground

1 teaspoon fresh thyme leaves, minced or pinch dry thyme

1 cup fresh cranberries

2 pork tenderloins, 10–12 ounces each

2 tablespoons extra virgin olive oil

Sauté onion in butter until it is translucent, then add honey, vinegar, wine, black pepper, thyme and cranberries. Bring to a boil, reduce heat and simmer until liquid is reduced, approximately 15 minutes. Set aside and keep warm.

Using a sharp knife remove all fat and silverskin from tenderloins. Slice almost in half horizontally and lay out flat. Between sheets of waxed paper pound with a meat mallet to 1/2 inch thickness. Spoon some confit over the tenderloins and roll up jelly-roll fashion. Secure rolls with butcher's twine.

Preheat oven to 375°F.

Brown on all sides in hot oil, then transfer to an overproof dish and bake until barely pink inside, about 20 minutes. Slice and serve over a bed of remaining warm confit.

Serves 4.

POACHED SALMON FILLET WITH CRANBERRY AND FENNEL RELISH

THE BRIARS RESORT, JACKSON'S POINT, ONT

At the Briars Resort chef Trevor Ledlie presents his salmon with boiled baby potatoes and a medley of snow peas. His relish or salsa adds colour contrasts to this appealing dish.

2 cups cranberries

1/4 cup water

2 cups diced fennel, inside parts only

1/4 teaspoon ground allspice

1/2 cup Japanese rice wine

1 tablespoon diced red onion

juice of 1 lime

1/2 teaspoon chopped jalapeno pepper

1 tablespoon chopped cilantro

salt and pepper, to taste

4 salmon fillets, boneless and skinless
(6 ounces each)

Cook cranberries in water until berries have popped and mixture thickens, approximately 8 minutes. Set aside and cool.

Remove outer layers of fennel and dice. In a bowl combine cranberries, fennel, allspice, rice wine, onion, lime juice, jalapeno and cilantro. Season with salt and pepper and refrigerate at least 4 hours.

Poach salmon fillets in a basic court bouillon, allowing 8 minutes per inch of thickness. To serve, place relish on plate, top with a salmon fillet and circle with accompanying vegetables.

Serves 4.

FETTUCINI ANNAPOLIS

SUNSHINE ON MAIN CAFE AND BISTRO, ANTIGONISH, NS

Chef Mark Gabrieau sautés scallops and chicken with cranberries and pesto, then flambés with vodka before adding heavy cream to thicken this pasta sauce. Pesto is available in jars in most large supermarkets, however, it is easily prepared at home.

1 1/2 tablespoons extra virgin olive oil

2 chicken breasts, boneless and skinless (4 ounces each)

1/4 pound bay scallops

2 tablespoons oil packed sun-dried tomatoes, chopped

2 tablespoons sun-dried cranberries

1 tablespoon pesto, recipe follows

1 teaspoons green pepper corns, drained

2 tablespoons diced apple

2 tablespoons vodka

2 tablespoons white wine

3/4 cup heavy cream (35% m.f.)

6 ounces fettucini, cooked al dente

salt and freshly ground pepper, to taste

grated parmesan cheese, as garnish

chopped parsley, as garnish

Heat oil in a large sauté pan over medium high heat. Slice chicken into bite-sized pieces. Add chicken, scallops, tomatoes, cranberries, pesto, diced apple and green peppercorns. Sauté quickly for 1 minute. Season with salt and pepper and flambé with vodka, then stir in white wine. Add cream and toss with warm pasta. Simmer until cream reduces enough to lightly coat the pasta noodles. Divide between 2 serving plates and sprinkle with parmesan cheese and parsley. Serves 2.

Pesto (supplied by author)

1/4 cup pine nuts

2 cups fresh basil, washed and stems removed (about 3 bunches)

4 large sprigs parsley, stems removed

2–3 cloves garlic, minced

1/4 cup Parmesan cheese

1/2 teaspoon pepper, freshly ground

1/2 cup extra virgin olive oil

Place pine nuts, basil, parsley, garlic, cheese and pepper in a food processor fitted with a metal blade. Process until mixture is finely chopped and smooth. With processor running, add oil in a thin stream. Process a further few seconds. Store leftover pesto in a sterilized jar and cover top with a thin layer of olive oil. Cover tightly and refrigerate for up to two months or freeze up to one year.

Yields 1 cup.

An innovative combination, Fettucini Annapolis, as created by chef Mark Gabrieau ▶ of Sunshine on Main Café and Bistro, Antigonish, NS

CROWN ROAST OF SPRING LAMB WITH DRIED-CRANBERRY JUS

SHADOW LAWN INN, ROTHESAY, NB

Chef Patricia Bullock of Shadow Lawn Inn advises that should your butcher not be able to "french" fresh lamb for you, well trimmed frozen racks are available in most supermarkets.

4 racks spring lamb, 7–8 ounces each

2 tablespoons canola oil

2 tablespoons butter

1/2 medium onion, minced

1 stalk celery, minced

2 cups bread cubes

1/4 cup dried apricots, diced

1/4 cup dried cranberries

pinch ground cloves

1/2 teaspoon rosemary, crumbled

small pinch dried thyme

salt and freshly ground pepper, to taste

Dried Cranberry Jus, recipe follows

Heat oil in a skillet over medium high heat and sear lamb racks, one at a time, turning once. Remove to a platter and keep warm.

Using a deep skillet, melt butter and sauté onion and celery slowly until transparent. Add bread cubes, apricots, cranberries, cloves, rosemary and thyme, stirring to combine. Season with salt and pepper and set aside.

Preheat oven to 400°F. Place each lamb rack on a cutting board, bone side down. With a very sharp knife slice part way through the loin of each rib. Using the photo as a guide, stand ribs on end, curling the rack into a crown with the meaty chops facing out. Tie each rack with a piece of butcher's twine to help it keep its shape, then place on a baking sheet. Repeat the procedure until you have 4 lamb crowns. Fill the centre of each crown with the stuffing. Roast lamb, 15 minutes for medium rare to 25 minutes for well done.

To serve, pour Dried Cranberry Jus over each serving plate. Remove string that is securing the crown roasts and place lamb in the centre of the plate. Surround with vegetables. Serves 4.

Dried-Cranberry Jus

1 cup full bodied red wine
e.g. Cabernet Sauvignon or Merlot

1 cup cranberry juice

1/4 cup dried cranberries

1 stalk fresh rosemary

2 cups beef broth

1 tablespoon cornstarch dissolved in
1 1/2 tablespoons water

salt and pepper, to taste

Place wine, juice, dried cranberries and rosemary in a saucepan over medium heat. Reduce until 1/2 cup liquid is remaining; discard rosemary. Add stock and simmer 15 minutes. Dissolve cornstarch in water and add to sauce. Continue simmering until sauce is clear and shiny. Season with salt and pepper, if desired.

*An impressive entrée for entertaining, Crown Roast of Spring Lamb as served at the ▶
Shadow Lawn Country Inn, in Rothsay, NB*

ROASTED GALLIANO CHICKEN WITH CRANBERRY CREAM SAUCE

DUNDEE ARMS HOTEL, CHARLOTTETOWN, PEI

Chef Austin Clement of the Dundee Arms Hotel elegantly flambés chicken with anise-flavoured Galliano before serving it with a creamy cranberry sauce.

1/4 cup vegetable oil

4 chicken breasts, bone in and skin attached

flour for dredging

3 tablespoons butter

1/2 cup chopped leeks

6 tablespoons Galliano liqueur

1/2 cup cranberry sauce

1 cup heavy cream (35% m.f.)

Preheat oven to 375°F.

Heat oil in a metal baking dish over medium high heat. Dust chicken with flour and sear allowing 1–2 minutes per side. Finish off in oven and bake until chicken is cooked and juices run clear, approximately 15–20 minutes. Remove chicken to a warm plate, tent with foil and let rest.

Place roasting pan over medium high heat, add butter and melt, stirring to remove any brown particles from the bottom of the pan. Add leeks and sauté 3 minutes, stirring constantly. Remove pan from heat, stir in Galliano and flambé. Add cranberry sauce and cream, return to heat and simmer to reduce and thicken.

To serve, arrange chicken on plates and nap with cranberry sauce. Serves 4.

Roasted Galliano Chicken with Cranberry Cream Sauce from the Dundee Arms ▶
Hotel, Charlottetown, PEI

BREAST OF DUCK SALAD WITH WARM VINAIGRETTE

LA MAISON DINING ROOM, HALIFAX, NS

At La Maison, Chef Karl-Heinz Szielasko serves braised duck with a salad of mixed greens, topped with a drizzle of warm vinaigrette.

1/2 cup red wine

1/4 cup brandy

2 tablespoons liquid honey

1/2 teaspoon minced garlic

1/4 teaspoon minced fresh ginger

1 teaspoon Worcestershire sauce

1/4 cup olive oil

1/4 cup chopped sun-dried cranberries

pinch cinnamon

pinch ground allspice

4 duck breasts, 4 ounces each

2 tablespoons olive oil

Mesclun greens to serve 4

12 cherry tomatoes

1 carrot, in julienne strips

1/2 small zucchini, in julienne strips

1/2 English style cucumber, thinly sliced

4 mushrooms, sliced

12–16 fresh cranberries, as garnish

In a large bowl whisk together wine, brandy, honey, garlic, ginger. Worcestershire sauce, oil, sun-dried cranberries, cinnamon and allspice. Place duck in marinade and let stand, refrigerated, overnight.

Preheat oven to 400°F.

Heat oil in an ovenproof pan over medium high heat and sear duck, turning once. Remove from burner, add marinade and cover. Bake until marinade is bubbly and duck is cooked, approximately 15 minutes.

While duck is baking, prepare 4 salad plates with greens and vegetables. Remove duck from pan and slice very thinly. Arrange over salads and drizzle with warm marinade. Garnish each plate with 3 or 4 fresh cranberries, which have been squeezed until they pop open slightly.

Serves 4.

Tender Breast of Duck Salad served with assorted vegetables at La Maison, Halifax, NS ▶

GRILLED VENISON WITH CRANBERRY CHUTNEY

INN AT BAY FORTUNE, BAY FORTUNE, PEI

For the photo presentation, chef Michael Smith served this dish with carrot napoleons and roast shallot vanilla jus. To fully appreciate his expertise, you may watch Chef Smith on his weekly cooking show entitled "The Inn Chef" on Life Channel.

1 cup Cabernet Sauvignon, or other full bodied red wine

2 cloves of garlic, finely minced

1 tablespoon Dijon mustard

2 tablespoons extra virgin olive oil

1/2 teaspoon ground allspice

1/2 teaspoon freshly ground black pepper

1 teaspoon salt

1 loin roast of venison, 1 1/2 to 2 pounds

rosemary sprigs, as garnish

Cranberry chutney, recipe follows

Place wine in a saucepan and bring to a boil, reduce heat and simmer until reduced to 2 tablespoons. Let cool. Whisk together the wine, garlic, mustard, allspice, pepper and salt, forming a marinade. Rub the venison roast with the marinade and refrigerate for 12 hours, allowing the flavours to perfume the meat.

Preheat oven to 350°F. Roast meat on a rack until it reaches medium rare, about 30–45 minutes. Allow roast to rest, covered, in a warm place for 15 minutes before slicing. Slice venison and arrange on plates. Garnish with Cranberry Chutney and a rosemary sprig.

Serves 4.

Cranberry Chutney

2 cups cranberries

1 large red onion, minced

2 cloves garlic, minced

1/2 cup sugar

1/2 cup red wine vinegar

1/2 teaspoon ground ginger

1/2 teaspoon ground allspice

1 teaspoon salt

1 teaspoon Tabasco sauce

Place all ingredients in a thick-bottomed saucepan and bring to a simmer. Reduce heat and cook, stirring frequently, until mixture thickens. Set aside.

Grilled Venison, the creation of chef Michael Smith of Inn at Bay Fortune, PEI ▶

PEAR AND CHEESE STUFFED CHICKEN BREASTS WITH DRIED-CRANBERRY BRANDY CREAM

WHITMAN INN, KEMPT, NS

Chef John Theiss intuitively knows which herbs and flavours complement one another. This recipe is an example of the epicurean delights to be found at Whitman Inn.

4 chicken breasts, boneless and skinless,

salt and pepper, to taste

1 teaspoon chopped parsley

1/2 teaspoon chopped rosemary

2 ounces smoked Gruyère cheese

2 ounces Emmentaler cheese

2 ounces medium cheddar cheese

1 ripe pear

flour for dredging

2 tablespoons butter

2 tablespoons vegetable oil

1/2 cup onion, chopped

1 large garlic clove, minced

1/2 cup Portobello or button mushrooms, chopped

1/4 teaspoon thyme

1/2 cup Chablis

1/2 cup chicken broth

1 bay leaf

3/4 cup sun-dried cranberries

salt and pepper, to taste

1/2 cup heavy cream (35% m.f.)

2 tablespoons brandy, optional

fresh cranberries, as garnish

parsley sprigs, as garnish

Flatten chicken breasts between pieces of plastic wrap to about 3/4-inch thickness. Sprinkle with salt, pepper, parsley and rosemary. Cut each piece of cheese into 4 pieces, 1/2 x 1 inch. Slice pear into 8 pieces, 1/4 x 1 inch each. Place two pieces of pear and one of each type of cheese in the centre of each chicken breast. Roll up carefully, securing with toothpicks. Dredge in flour, shaking off excess and brown in butter and oil over medium heat. Remove to a pan and keep warm. Pour off all but 1 tablespoon of remaining oil.

Sauté the onion and garlic for 2–3 minutes in the reserved oil. Add the mushrooms and sauté an additional 5 minutes. Sprinkle with thyme and deglaze pan with Chablis. Add chicken broth, bay leaf and cranberries, bring to a boil and reduce by 1/2 until very thick and cranberries are rehydrated but not mushy. Season with salt and pepper. Stir in cream and cook down to a thick sauce. Remove from heat and add brandy, if desired.

Preheat oven to 350° F. Spoon sauce over chicken breasts and bake covered in an ovenproof pan 15 minutes. Remove cover and bake an additional 10–15 minutes until chicken is done. Garnish platter with a few fresh cranberries and parsley sprigs. Serves 4.

Pear and Cheese Stuffed Chicken Breasts with Dried-Cranberry Brandy Cream, ▶
Whitman Inn, Kempt, NS

ROAST BREAST OF PHEASANT IN A DRIED-CRANBERRY JUS

THE HALLIBURTON HOUSE INN, HALIFAX, NS

On his extensive menu, chef Scott Vail of Halliburton House Inn features several wild game selections. This is a mild-flavoured dish and sure to please the most discerning palate.

4 pheasant breasts, deboned

1 teaspoon fresh rosemary, finely chopped

1 teaspoon extra virgin olive oil

2 bay leaves

1/2 teaspoons freshly grated black pepper

1/4 teaspoon salt

4 tablespoons sweet butter, divided

2 shallots, finely diced

1/3 cup dried cranberries

1 teaspoon balsamic vinegar

2 tablespoons white port

2 cups pheasant or chicken stock

Rinse and pat dry pheasant breasts. In a shallow dish combine rosemary, olive oil, bay leaves and black pepper. Roll breasts in mixture and cover. Refrigerate for 4 hours.

Preheat oven to 325°F.

Melt 1 tablespoon of butter in a sauté pan and brown breasts, turning once. Remove meat to a baking dish and roast until just pink, 12–15 minutes.

While pheasant is roasting sauté shallots in 1 tablespoon of butter until soft, approximately 5 minutes, add cranberries and sauté 1 additional minute. Deglaze pan with balsamic vinegar and port and reduce until dry. Stir in stock and bring to a full boil, lower heat and reduce slightly. Remove from heat and whisk in remaining butter. Serve breasts napped with Cranberry Jus.

Serves 4.

Roast Breast of Duck in Dried Cranberry Jus as presented by the chef of ▶
Halliburton House Inn, Halifax, NS.

SEASONS' CRANBERRY GLAZED CHICKEN

SEASONS IN THYME, SUMMERSIDE, PEI

This is possibly one of the tastiest chicken recipes you will find. While you may choose any type of potato or vegetable, chef Stephan Czapalay suggests medium flavoured vegetables to complement the chicken. Why not try basil sautéed carrots and pattypan squash, or sautéed spinach? He suggests a dry heat method for potatoes, such as roasted whole potatoes or herb roasted new potatoes.

4 chicken breasts, skin on and wishbone attached

12 fresh sage or basil leaves

salt and pepper, to season

3 tablespoons olive oil

Season's Cranberry Glaze, recipe follows

Rinse chicken breasts and pat them dry . Gently lift the skin and slide in 3 or 4 herb leaves so that they lie flat between the skin and the breast. Season breasts with salt and pepper.

Preheat oven to 350°F.

Place a sauté pan over high heat and add oil. Gently place the breasts in the pan, skin side down and sauté approximately 3-5 minutes until skin is golden. Turn and sauté an additional 3 minutes. Remove breasts and finish off in oven, 10-15 minutes. Allow to rest 4-6 minutes before carving.

Drizzle with Season's Cranberry Glaze.

Serves 4.

Season's Cranberry Glaze

1/2 tablespoon olive oil

1 tablespoon finely diced shallots

1/2 tablespoon finely chopped orange zest

1/4 cup whole cranberries

1/4 cup white wine

2 cups chicken stock

1 tablespoon unsalted butter

salt and pepper, to taste

Heat oil in a small saucepan over medium high heat. Add shallots and sauté approximately 1 1/2 minutes, being careful not to brown. Add zest, cranberries and white wine; reduce by half. Add stock and reduce by 2/3. Swirl in butter with a small whisk, season with salt and pepper.

Chef Stephan Czapalay presents his Seasons' Cranberry Glazed Chicken at ▶
Seasons in Thyme Restaurant, Summerside, PEI

HERB CRUSTED PORK TENDERLOIN WITH CRANBERRY COMPOTE

BLOMIDON INN, WOLFVILLE, NS

Blomidon Inn's chef, Keith Bond, recognizes the versatility of cranberries. In this pork entrée he balances the flavours of the tart berries with sweet valley apples and finishes the plate with roasted potatoes and a medley of colourful vegetables.

1 pork tenderloin, 16–18 ounce size

2 tablespoons Dijon-style mustard

2 teaspoons liquid honey

1/4 cup dried breadcrumbs

1/4 teaspoon freshly grated black pepper

1/4 teaspoon salt

2 teaspoons chopped fresh herbs,
e.g., rosemary, thyme, oregano,

Cranberry Compote, recipe follows

Preheat oven to 325°F.

Trim all fat, tissue and silverskin from tenderloin.

In a small bowl combine mustard and honey and rub over tenderloin.

In a separate bowl combine crumbs, pepper, salt and herbs. Gently coat tenderloin with herb mixture and place on a rack in a roasting pan. Bake until tenderloin is nicely browned and barely pink inside, approximately 45 minutes. Remove to a warm platter and let rest a few minutes before slicing into medallions.

Serve with Cranberry Compote.

Serves 4.

Cranberry Compote

1 cup water

2 cups sugar

2 cups cranberries

2 cups chopped apple

In a large saucepan combine water and sugar, stirring until sugar has dissolved. Bring to a boil, reduce heat and simmer 5 minutes. Stir in cranberries and apples and return to a boil. Remove from heat, cool then refrigerate.

Herb Crusted Pork Tenderloin served in the dining room of Blomidon Inn, Wolfville, NS ▶

DESSERTS

*C*ranberries are truly a versatile berry, and like strawberries and blueberries, bring out the creative side in every chef. The desserts we offer here are as tempting as any to be found in the best restaurants and inns.

◄ *Cranberry in a Hazelnut Tart, the creation of chef Whitney Armstrong of Catherine McKinnon's Spot O'Tea Restaurant, Stanley Bridge, PEI*

CRANBERRY IN A HAZELNUT TART

CATHERINE MCKINNON'S SPOT O' TEA RESTAURANT, STANLEY BRIDGE, PEI

Created by pastry chef Whitney Armstrong, the tarts may be made using fresh or frozen cranberries. For the photo presentation, he served the tarts accompanied by poached apple slices.

1/2 cup butter

1/4 cup sugar

1 small egg

1 cup flour

2 tablespoons ground hazelnuts

Grand Marnier Orange Sauce, recipe follows

Cranberry Filling, recipe follows

Cream together butter and sugar until fluffy. Add egg, flour and hazelnuts and continue to beat until well blended. Chill in refrigerator 1/2 hour. Roll out on a lightly floured surface and cut in circles to fill eight 3-inch tart molds. Chill again for 1/2 hour.

Preheat oven to 375 °F. Bake tarts until they are firm and a light brown colour, approximately 12 minutes. Remove from oven, cool and unmold.

To serve, spoon Cranberry Filling into tart shells. Spread a little Grand Marnier Orange Sauce over serving plates and top with tarts. Serves 8.

Grand Marnier Orange Sauce

1/2 tablespoon cornstarch

1 tablespoon sugar

1/2 cup orange juice

2 tablespoons Grand Marnier liqueur

In a small saucepan combine cornstarch and sugar. Whisk in orange juice and bring to a boil. Reduce heat and simmer, stirring constantly until sauce is thickened. Remove from burner and stir in Grand Marnier. Cool to room temperature.

Cranberry Filling

3 cups fresh or frozen cranberries

1/2 cup raspberries

1 cup sugar

1 cup red cranberry jelly

zest of 1 orange, finely grated

1 tablespoons gelatin dissolved in 3 tablespoons cold water

Combine cranberries, raspberries, sugar, jelly and zest in a large saucepan and cook over medium high heat until cranberries are softened and sugar is dissolved. Remove from heat and stir in dissolved gelatin. Return to heat and cook mixture until gelatin is completely incorporated. Transfer to a bowl and refrigerate.

CRANBERRY MAPLE BREAD PUDDING

INN ON THE COVE, SAINT JOHN, NB

Innkeepers Willa and Ross Mavis serve traditional bread pudding which takes on a new zing with the addition of cranberries and maple syrup. They also vary the recipe by using blueberries in season. Whipped cream or a creamy chocolate sauce turns bread pudding into gourmet fare.

5 slices white bread, lightly buttered on both sides

4 tablespoons fresh cranberries

2 tablespoons mincemeat

3/4 cup heavy cream (35% m.f.)

3/4 cup milk

pinch of salt

2 tablespoons sugar

1 teaspoon vanilla

2 eggs, lightly beaten

4 teaspoons pure maple syrup

1/2 cup heavy cream (35% m.f.), whipped

2 tablespoons pure maple syrup, as garnish

Preheat oven to 375°F.

Choose four round baking dishes or ramekins about 3 1/2 inches in diameter. Grease dishes lightly with butter. Using a cookie cutter the same size as the base of each ramekin, cut a circle out of 4 pieces of buttered bread. Place these rounds in the bottom of each container.

Retain the crusts and bread scraps and together with the remaining slice of bread, slice into cubes. Sprinkle the cranberries and mincemeat equally on top of the bread rounds and cover with the cubed bread pieces. Do not pack the bread cubes, but fill each container to its rim.

In a small saucepan over medium heat, combine cream, milk, salt and sugar and whisk well. Heat to just boiling. Remove from burner, stir in vanilla and quickly whisk in beaten eggs.

Drizzle maple syrup over bread in each ramekin and fill to the top with heated milk mixture. Place ramekins in shallow pan, pour boiling water into pan half way up the sides of the dishes. Bake until custard is set, approximately 45 minutes.

Serve warm with whipped cream and a further drizzle of maple syrup. Serves 4.

PEERLESS CRANBERRY CARROT CAKE

WICKWIRE HOUSE, KENTVILLE, NS

After many variations, this recipe has been perfected by innkeeper Darlene Peerless. I'm sure it will become your best-ever carrot cake recipe too!

4 cups grated carrots

2 cups sugar

1 cup butter, cut in pieces

1 can crushed pineapple in unsweetened juice, 14-ounce size

3 cups flour

1/2 teaspoon double-acting baking powder

2 teaspoons baking soda

1 tablespoon cinnamon

2 teaspoons cloves

1 teaspoon allspice

1 teaspoon nutmeg

1/2 teaspoon salt

1 cup dried cranberries

2 eggs

Cream Cheese Frosting, recipe follows

Preheat oven to 350°F.

In a medium saucepan bring carrots, sugar, butter and pineapple with juice to a simmer, then cook 5 minutes, stirring occasionally. Remove from burner and cool completely.

Combine flour, baking powder, baking soda, cinnamon, cloves, allspice, nutmeg, salt and cranberries in a large bowl.

In a separate large bowl beat eggs until lemon coloured, then add carrot mixture and stir to combine. Add flour mixture, stirring only until batter is combined. Pour into a greased and floured 10-inch bundt or tube pan and bake approximately 45 minutes or until a toothpick inserted in the centre comes out clean.

Remove from oven and let stand 10 minutes before turning out onto a serving plate. Cover with Cream Cheese Frosting.

Serves 10–12.

Cream Cheese Frosting

1 package cream cheese, 8-ounce size, softened,

1/2 cup butter, softened

2 cups icing sugar, sifted

1/2 cup pecans, chopped

1/2 cup crushed pineapple, well drained

1/4 cup dried cranberries, chopped

With an electric mixer combine cheese, butter and icing sugar. Beat until light and fluffy. Stir in remaining ingredients.

The ultimate carrot cake, Peerless Cranberry Carrot Cake as served by innkeeper ▶ Darlene Peerless of Wickwire House, Kentville, NS

BRANT'S PIE

CHARLOTTE LANE CAFE & CRAFTS, SHELBURNE, NS

At the Charlotte Lane, chef Glauser prepares this pie with a lattice topping. For the photo he served it on a bed of Crème Anglâise with Raspberry Coulis hearts!

1 cup fresh orange juice

2/3 cup sugar

2 cups fresh cranberries

1/2 large pear, cut in 1/4 inch dice

1/2 large Macintosh apple, cut in 1/4 inch dice

1 tablespoon cornstarch dissolved in 2 tablespoons cold water

pastry of choice for a 2-crust pie

icing sugar for dusting

whipped cream or crème fraîche*

Combine orange juice, sugar, cranberries, pear and apple in a large saucepan and bring to a boil over medium high heat. Reduce temperature and simmer until fruit is soft and cranberries have popped. Dissolve cornstarch in cold water and stir into cranberry mixture. Cook until filling has thickened. Remove from the burner, cool, then refrigerate several hours.

Preheat oven to 350°F.

Prepare pastry recipe of choice and divide in two. Roll out and use half of it to line a shallow 8-inch pie plate. Pour in chilled pie filling.

Roll out the second half of pastry. Cut in 3/4x12-inch strips and lay these on pie at 1-intervals. Fold back alternate strips to weave crosswise strips over and under for a lattice top. Bake in preheated oven until lightly brown, approximately 35–40 minutes. Cool well and dust with icing sugar.

Serve with a dollop of whipped cream or crème fraîche. Serves 6.

* Crème Fraîche is a mature, thickened cream that is easy to prepare and will keep refrigerated for up to one week. Simply place 1 cup heavy cream (35% m.f.) in a glass bowl, stir in 2 tablespoons buttermilk and cover. Allow to stand at room temperature approximately 70°F, 8–24 hours. Stir well, cover and refrigerate.

A cranberry delight, Brants Pie, served with flair by Chef Roland Glauser of ▶ Charlotte Lane Café and Crafts, Shelburne, NS

APPLE CRANBERRY PIE

AUX ANCIENS CANADIENS
RESTAURANT, QUEBEC CITY, QUE

This straightforward recipe is a tasty variation on an old theme. The chef suggests serving it warm with a generous scoop of good quality vanilla ice cream.

pastry for a 2-crust pie

1 cup fresh or frozen cranberries, quartered

4 medium apples, peeled, cored and thinly sliced

1 1/4 cups sugar

1 tablespoon flour

1 teaspoon ground nutmeg

Preheat oven to 375°F.

Prepare pastry recipe of choice and line a 9-inch pie plate.

In a large bowl combine cranberries and apple slices. In a separate bowl stir together the sugar, flour and nutmeg. Pour sugar mixture over cranberries and toss to coat. Place in prepared pie plate, cover with remaining pastry round and cut a few vent holes in pie crust.

Bake until crust is brown and fruit is bubbly, approximately 35–40 minutes.

Serves 6.

CRANBERRY SORBET

BLOMIDON INN, WOLFVILLE, NS

Assorted fruit sorbets are often served between courses at the Blomidon Inn as palate refreshers. For this presentation, Cranberry Sorbet has been served on a bed of Crème de Menthe liqueur, making it an excellent choice for a festive light dessert.

2 cups sugar

1 cup water

3/4 cup pure cranberry juice

Crème de Menthe liqueur, optional

fresh mint sprigs, as garnish

Combine sugar and water in a large saucepan and stir until the sugar is dissolved. Bring to a boil over medium high heat, reduce temperature and simmer 5 minutes. Remove from burner, stir in cranberry juice and cool.

Process mixture in an electric ice cream maker following manufacturer's instructions, then place in a covered plastic container and freeze. Serve a small scoop of sorbet over a bed of Crème de Menthe liqueur, garnished with fresh mint sprigs. Serves 6.

Cool and smooth, Blomidon Inn's Cranberry Sorbet is served ▶ on a bed of Crème de Menthe liqueur

MAPLE SYRUP MOUSSE WITH CRANBERRY COULIS

LA PERLA DINING ROOM, DARTMOUTH, NS

In this colourful dessert Chef James MacDougall of La Perla combines the sweet flavours of maple syrup mousse with the semi-tart flavour of fresh cranberry coulis.

1 tablespoon unflavoured gelatin

2 tablespoons cold water

1 cup pure maple syrup

1 cup heavy cream (35% m.f.), whipped

1 tablespoon brandy

Cranberry Coulis, recipe follows

Candied Cranberries, recipe follows

Additional whipped cream, as garnish

Soften gelatin in cold water, approximately 5 minutes. Place in the top part of a double boiler over simmering water until dissolved.

In a separate saucepan bring maple syrup to a boil and pour over dissolved gelatin. Stir to combine, remove from heat and cool.

While syrup is cooling, whip cream to soft peaks. When syrup is cool, but not set, stir in the brandy and then fold in the whipped cream. Pour into 6 individual ramekins and chill until set.

To serve, drizzle Cranberry Coulis over six dessert plates. Carefully unmold the mousses and place on the sauce. Garnish with a rosette of whipped cream and a few Candied Cranberries.

Serves 6.

Cranberry Coulis

2 cups fresh cranberries

2/3 cup butter

2/3 cup caster (superfine) sugar

1 1/2 tablespoon brandy

Combine cranberries and water in a large saucepan and boil for 10 minutes. Pass through a sieve and reserve juices. Return juice to a boil, stir in sugar and boil to reduce slightly, approximately 3 minutes. Remove all foam from syrup, stir in brandy and cool.

Candied Cranberries

12 large fresh cranberries

egg white from one large egg

1/2 cup caster (superfine) sugar

In a small bowl, whisk egg white until frothy. Toss in cranberries to coat. Roll cranberries in sugar and dry on a piece of waxed paper.

Maple Syrup Mousse with Cranberry Coulis, the work of ▶
chef James MacDougall of La Perla, Dartmouth, NS

STEAMED CRANBERRY PUDDING WITH BUTTERSCOTCH SAUCE

THE MURRAY MANOR BED AND BREAKFAST, YARMOUTH, NS

Innkeeper Joan Semple acquired this delightful dessert recipe during a sojourn in Colorado.

1/2 cup molasses

2 teaspoons baking soda

1/2 cup hot water

1 cup fresh whole cranberries

1 1/3 cup flour

1 teaspoon baking powder

Butterscotch Sauce, recipe follows

In a mixing bowl beat together the molasses and baking soda. Slowly add the hot water.

Sift together flour and baking powder and stir into the molasses mixture, making a dough. Fold in cranberries and pour into a greased steaming mold. Cover and steam 2 1/2 hours.

Serve warm with Butterscotch Sauce.
Serves 6–8.

Butterscotch Sauce

1/2 cup butter

1/2 cup blend or half and half cream (10% m.f.)

1 cup brown sugar

1 teaspoon vanilla

Combine all ingredients in a saucepan and bring to a boil. Reduce heat and simmer 5 minutes. Serve warm.

CHRISTMAS MARGARITAS

THE ACTOR'S RETREAT CAFÉ, VICTORIA, PEI

Olé! Chef Paul Sheridan prepares this Margarita base several weeks before he serves his Christmas Margaritas... but why wait for Christmas?

4 cups fresh cranberries

2 cups sugar

2 cups Tequila (or Gin)

Chop cranberries, then add with sugar to Tequila. Place in a glass jar with a non-metallic lid. Shake once daily for three weeks. Strain mixture through a fine sieve, pressing lightly on any solids to squeeze out juice. Serve over crushed ice. Yields 3 cups.

Christmas Margaritas, a seasonal favourite at the Actor's Retreat Café, Victoria, PEI ▶

PUFFS FILLED WITH CRANBERRY CREAM

LITTLE SHEMOQUE COUNTRY INN, PORT ELGIN, NB

*Innkeeper Petra Sudbrack offers her guests the best of local fruits and vegetables.
These cranberry-filled cream puffs are an example of her innovative talents.*

1 cup flour

1/4 teaspoon salt

pinch of freshly grated nutmeg

3/4 cup water

1 cup butter, cut in 6 equal pieces

3 eggs

2 cups cranberries

2/3 cup sugar

water

3 tablespoons Cointreau liqueur

1 cup heavy cream (35% m.f.), whipped

icing sugar for dusting

chocolate syrup for drizzling, optional

Preheat oven to 400°F.

Grease a large baking sheet and set aside.

Sift flour, salt and nutmeg onto a sheet of waxed paper or foil.

In a medium saucepan bring the water and butter to a boil. Remove from heat and add the dry ingredients all at once. Beat with a wooden spoon for about 1 minute, until well blended, and mixture starts to pull away from the sides of the saucepan. Set the saucepan over low heat and cook mixture for about 2 minutes, beating constantly. Remove from heat. Add the eggs, one at a time, beating well after each addition to make a smooth, shiny dough.

Using a tablespoon, ease the dough into 12 mounds on prepared baking sheet. Bake 25–30 minutes. Remove puffs from oven and cut a small slit in them to release the steam. Turn off thermostat and leave oven door ajar. Return puffs to oven to dry.

While puffs are baking combine cranberries, sugar and add enough water to cover berries in a medium saucepan. Heat at medium setting until berries are very soft, approximately 20 minutes. Remove from heat and stir in Cointreau. Set aside to cool, then refrigerate.

To serve, fold whipped cream into chilled cranberries. Spoon into puffs, dust with icing sugar and drizzle with chocolate syrup.

Yields 12–14 Puffs.

Puffs filled with Cranberry Cream from Little Shemoque Country Inn, Port Elgin, NB ▶

INDEX